D0381248

JUST FOR
KICKS!

JUST FOR KICKS!

600 KNOCK-OUT JOKES, PUNS & RIDDLES ABOUT SPORTS

JOHN BRIGGS

STERLING CHILDREN'S BOOKS
New York

To Max, Bill, & Bob — for
keeping baseball fun

STERLING CHILDREN'S BOOKS
New York

An Imprint of Sterling Publishing Co., Inc.
1166 Avenue of the Americas
New York, NY 10036

ISBN 978-1-4549-3045-7

Distributed in Canada by Sterling Publishing Co., Inc.
c/o Canadian Manda Group, 664 Annette Street
Toronto, Ontario M6S 2C8, Canada
Distributed in the United Kingdom by GMC Distribution Services
Castle Place, 166 High Street, Lewes, East Sussex BN7 1XU, England
Distributed in Australia by NewSouth Books
45 Beach Street, Coogee, NSW 2034, Australia

For information about custom editions, special sales, and premium and
corporate purchases, please contact Sterling Special Sales at 800-805-5489
or specialsales@sterlingpublishing.com.

Manufactured in Canada

Lot #:
2 4 6 8 10 9 7 5 3 1
08/18

sterlingpublishing.com

Contents

WARM-UPS

Knock, knock!

KNOCK-KNOCK!

> Who's there?

Ostrich.

> Ostrich who?

Ostrich before I go running.

Why do soccer players have fun during warm-ups?

> They're getting their kicks.

Why can't you play baseball in the snow?

> The pitchers can't warm up.

Which player never gets loose before a game?

> The tight end.

Why do high jumpers practice in April?

> It's *spring* training.

Why don't athletes look for clams?

> They might pull a mussel.

FUNGOES FOR EVERYONE

What did the baseball say to the catcher?

"So, we mitt again."

What was the last thing the shortstop heard before he hurt his head?

A screaming line drive.

Why did the fielder check the baseball for glasses?

She thought the ball must have eyes on it.

What does a shortstop like to read?

A pop-up book.

When can a penny save you from a foul ball?

When it's "Heads up!"

Why didn't the Jedi tag the runner?

It was a force out.

What do you call a dad from Georgia?

A South pa.

Why did the young baseball player bring a soda bottle to the game?

To prove he had *pop*.

Why did the shortstop feel stupid playing in a dome?

It was inside baseball.

What did the infielder say when the game got boring?

"Where did the fungo?"

Why did the baseball player come home early from his date?

He struck out.

Why does baseball have so many curses?

If you missed the ball two out of three times, you'd curse, too.

How do you give directions to a baseball player?

"Make three lefts and you're home."

Why don't catchers pay rent?

They're squatters.

HA HA HA HA HA HA HA HA

Why does an outfielder throw thick rugs over bugs?

To shag some flies.

Why can't you trust a softball pitch?

It's underhanded.

Why is a baseball team off-balance?

They have no center.

What game involves the entire universe?

The All-Star Game.

When does a baseball team have a lot of players who work for the power company?

When it's filled with utility players.

Why did the third basemen join the army?

He had a cannon for an arm.

Why do outfielders play the drums?

Because they can't play the base.

What game makes baseball players sneeze?

Pepper.

Where's the perfect place to plant flowers?

Scenterfield.

Why did the baseball team send its three oldest players to a nursing home?

They retired the side.

How does lettuce slide into second?

Head first.

How does a ruler slide into second?

Feet first.

Where do you place a baserunner whose legs have turned to jelly?

On the injured preserve.

Did you hear about the baseball player's new song?

It's a hit.

What do hungry baseball players do?

Crowd the plate.

What do you call a baseball player who won't chase away flies?

Shoo-less Joe.

What's a catcher's favorite dessert?

Bunt cake.

How does a hitter make an error in baseball?

With a blooper.

Why do baserunners make so many mistakes?

They're way off base.

HERE BATTER, BATTER

Why do bad hitters have a good sense of smell?

They whiff a lot.

Why did the batter go on a diet?

He was tired of being a heavy hitter.

Why does the home-run hitter's dance go all night?

It's a long ball.

Why did the batter float over the stadium?

He was up.

Why do batters fall asleep in extra innings?

They're up late.

Why couldn't the batter get a hit after she lost her watch?

Her timing was off.

How does a pancake chef hit so many home runs?

With a strong batter.

What do you call a ballplayer who can turn on a lamp with either hand?

A light switch hitter.

When does a baseball player bring her bike to the game?

When she hits for the cycle.

Why did the home-run hitter work for the electric company?

He had power.

Which ballplayer has a spotless room?

The clean-up hitter.

HA HA HA HA HA

NOT A BELLY ITCHER

Why was the pitcher looking in the garbage?

He threw his arm out.

Why did the pitcher have so many great ideas?

She was spitballing.

Why couldn't the goofy pitcher throw a screwball?

He had a screw loose.

Why couldn't the pitcher throw a curveball?

She couldn't get the right angle.

Why should pitchers work for the cable company?

They have a splitter.

Why did the pitcher go in circles?

It was her turn in the rotation.

Why did the pitcher eat too much before the game?

He was set to hurl.

What do you call it when a baseball player throws an ad across the room?

A sales pitch.

Why were the pitcher and catcher charged up for the game?

They're a battery.

Why aren't pitchers popular in the summer?

They bring the heat.

How did the pitcher wear his pants?

High and tight.

What does a pitcher throw in the desert?

High heat.

Why was the baseball team's ace such a good singer?

She had perfect pitch.

How is a pitcher like a toy soldier?

They both wind up.

When is a pitcher like his best pitch?

When he's a screwball.

How does a soccer goalie start a play?

She gets the ball rolling.

What do you call a soccer field at a party?

A wild pitch.

Where do soccer players get sick?

At a fever pitch.

What do you call a soccer field with dead grass?

Pitch black.

Why do firefighters go to every soccer game?

In case one team throws the match.

What's the longest word in soccer?

Goooooooaaaaaaaallllllll!

Why can't midfielders learn sign language?

They can't use their hands.

HA HA HA HA HA

Why is it easy to insult the center back?

He's always defensive.

What did the soccer player say when his coach told him to score a goal?

"I'll pass."

Why did the soccer player have so much jewelry?

He was a gold keeper.

Why can't a soccer player who has said something embarrassing kick the ball?

He has his foot in his mouth.

Why did the foolish soccer player kick her tires?

She was doing a bicycle kick.

Why can't soccer players stay clean?

They all want to be Messi.

Why was the sweeper's house so dirty?

He didn't bring his work home.

HA HA HA HA HA
HA HA HA HA HA

FOURTH AND FUN

What is Captain Hook's favorite football play?

The handoff.

Why is Captain Hook such a good wide receiver?

He made a one-handed grab.

Which football player smells the best?

Right Guard.

Why did the punter wrap a rope around the football?

To get great hang time.

Why do landscapers make terrible running backs?

They only do one yard at a time.

Why do actors score so many points in football?

They're playmakers.

What does a wide receiver eat at a seafood restaurant?

The catch of the day.

When does an airplane pilot spike a football?

After touchdown.

Why did the football team hire a dessert chef?

They wanted to ice the kicker.

Why did the football team hire a giant lobster?

They needed a long snapper.

Why did the football player grab a ball on the Ferris wheel?

It was a fair catch.

Which football player can't lie down?

The halfback.

What's a wideout's favorite part of a wedding?

The reception.

How does a return man give a good massage?

With a touchback.

Why did the punter quit his job at the store?

Too many returns.

When is a football team like autumn leaves?

When they're in a pile.

In which month does the defense stop the most field goals?

Block-tober.

When is a football team like a bad hair day?

When they have split ends.

Which football player can't play games indoors?

Outside linebacker.

How do you pick up a heavy football player?

With a block and tackle.

What's the only thing that doesn't move at a football game?

The stay-dium.

Why couldn't the football team play in the back field?

It was in motion.

Why did the football stop moving?

It went *out of bounce.*

When can you march down the field in a football game?

When you're in the marching band.

How is dynamite like a star running back?

They're both explosive.

What's the safest drink for a football player?

Safe-tea.

Why was the cornerback so good?

He was in the zone.

Where did the safety get his quarter back?

In the pocket.

Why can you trust goalposts?

They're upright.

Why did the football player put on a sweater?

She was in the draft.

JOKE ONE, JOKE TWO . . . HIKE!

Why was the quarterback's hand wet?

He hit the showers.

How did the school quarterback hurt his hand?

He hit the books.

Why couldn't the sick quarterback throw downfield?

He could only throw up.

How does a quarterback in a rush like his eggs?

Scrambled.

Why did the quarterback bring a book to the game?

In case he was given the read option.

How does a quarterback stand in the pocket?

With tiny feet.

Why did the quarterback throw a clock at the wide receiver?

It was a timing route.

Who can't play football on Monday nights?

Monday morning quarterbacks.

Why did the quarterback use a butter knife?

He wanted to spread the defense.

How did the quarterback lose his job?

He got sacked.

Why did the quarterback take up ditch digging?

He wanted to make a shovel pass.

How did the football player get away with so many lies?

She was a quarterback sneak.

Which space alien makes a great quarterback?

Jabba the Hutt! Hutt! Hutt!

WHISTLEBLOWERS

What did the coach do when the baserunner got caught stealing?

She let it slide.

Why did the football coach lecture his team after every score?

He wanted to make a point after touchdown.

Why do coaches make lousy writers?

They spell everything X and O.

What did the coach tell his heavy hitter?

Donut swing for the fences.

Why did the softball coach think her players had crazy ideas?

They came out of left field.

Why did the football coach hire an artist?

For the draw play.

How much change does a coach get for his quarter?

A nickelback.

What's the one back a football coach doesn't like?

The talkback.

What did wrestling coach Nelson name his son?

Half Nelson.

Why did the coach put numbers on the stadium steps?

She wanted to run up the score.

Why do referees wear stripes and not spots?

Because they're not cheetahs.

What's black and white and red all over?

An embarrassed referee.

How can you tell when referees are happy?

They whistle while they work.

Which famous tourist attraction did the umpire visit in Italy?

The Roman Call-em-as-I-see-em.

Why do baseball umpires wear masks?

So they don't play faceball.

When does the referee yell at the clock?

When it's a two-minute warning.

What do you call a referee who loves a loud whistle?

A *shrill* seeker.

Why can't you trust a referee?

He's a whistle blower.

HA HA HA HA HA HA HA HA

Why wouldn't the umpire call a strike?

She wasn't in the union.

How does an umpire make pancakes fly?

"Batter up!"

HOOP HUMOR

Why did the magician like basketball?

He could make a trick shot.

What's the worst thing about playing basketball outdoors?

Every shot is an air ball.

Why can't two babies play basketball?

They double dribble.

Why did the basketball player kick the ball into the net?

He was going for a field goal.

HA HA HA HA HA

What did the women's basketball star wear to the party?

A hoop skirt.

Who is the sharpest player on a basketball team?

The point guard.

Why did the number one basketball team grow such big plants?

They had the highest seed.

What TV show is all about basketball uniforms?

ShortsCenter.

Why do basketball players play Horse?

Because Hippopotamus takes too long.

How did the teller get so many points?

Bank shots.

How do basketball players cool off?

They go for a dunk.

When is a basketball player like a fighter?

When he gets boxed out.

Why was the basketball player so bad at defense?

He didn't give a hoop.

Why did the basketball player bring a suitcase to the game?

In case she traveled.

What do you call a broken leg in the first quarter?

A fast break.

What did the basketball player have with dinner?

A finger roll.

Why did the basketball star get 6 scoops of ice cream?

She got a triple double.

ICEBREAKERS

What do you call a hockey player with all his teeth?

A rookie.

Why did the hockey star wrinkle his uniform?

So he could score in the crease.

What do parents call it when their young goalies leave home?

Empty Net Syndrome.

Why do moms make great goalies?

Nothing gets by them.

Why was the magician the best hockey player in the league?

She always had a hat trick.

Why did the genius never make a penalty in hockey?

He thought outside the box.

Why do hockey goalies make good presidents?

Because the puck stops here.

What do you call a great goal in hockey?

An ice shot.

How did the hockey team lose their big lead?

They had a meltdown.

How does a hockey team keep the lights on?

With a power play.

How can you tell when a hockey player is choosy?

He picks a fight.

What is an ice hockey player's favorite food?

Brrrrr-ito.

Who's the most popular player at a hockey game?

The bench warmer.

Which move makes an ice skater fall three times?

A triple klutz.

Why do figure skaters drive big cars?

They need a triple axel.

Where do tiny people skate?

An ice shrink.

Why did the speed skater carry a screwdriver?

To make tight turns.

When do you skate at a tiny rink?

When it's a rinky-dink.

How did the figure skater do on her test?

She slid by.

How did the curling team win the championship?

In a clean sweep.

How did the skier get hurt?

She hit the slopes.

Why did the skier think his career was over?

It was all downhill from there.

HOLE IN PUN

What did the golfer say when he swung too soon?

"Three!"

Why did the golfer yell "Five!"?

She hit the ball farther than four.

How do you insult a golfer?

With a *chip* shot.

Why did the golfer bring a clown with him on short shots?

He wanted to make a silly putty.

Why did the golfer take up badminton?

It was the only way she could get a birdy.

How much cake does a bad golfer eat?

Slice after slice.

How do you know when a bad golfer cuts the pizza?

All the slices go to the left.

How far did the golfer hit the ball?

A fair way.

Can any golfer make a hole in one?

It's a long shot.

What did the golfer say to the caddy carrying his golf bag?

"Putter anywhere."

Why did the golfer bring her Caddy on the field?

It was faster than the golf cart.

Why did the golfer ride a camel?

To get out of the sand trap.

Why did the golfer bring her clubs home?

She wanted to putter around the house.

Why did the golfer get an F in school?

He got the lowest score.

How can you tell when a golf ball is happy?

It has dimples.

What did the astronaut say to the golfer when he was two under par?

"The Eagle has landed."

What's the golf course on the moon made out of?

Astro-turf.

What did the scientist call the golf course she couldn't find?

The missing links.

Why are cavemen good at golf?

They bring their own clubs.

Knock, knock!

Who's there?

Putter.

Putter who?

Putter there, pal!

KNOCK-KNOCK!

PUNCH LINES

Why are boxers so good at telling jokes?

They never miss a punchline.

Why did the boxer take a train ride?

To get his ticket punched.

What did the boxer order after he lost the fight?

Spare ribs.

How does a boxer reach her destination?

She goes the distance.

What do you call a fighter in the desert?

A sand boxer.

Why did the boxer get a job at the post office?

He wanted to pack a punch.

How do boxers say hello?

Fist bump.

HA HA

HA HA HA

POW

What do you call someone texting at a boxing match?

Bored of the Rings.

What do you call someone sleeping at a boxing match?

Snored at the Rings.

Why did the boxer tie up the fool?

She wanted to rope a dope.

What does a boxer say when serving tea?

One lump or two.

Why was the losing boxer such a good dancer?

He got the beat down.

How did the lollipop win the fight?

With a sucker punch.

Why did the boxer wear a coat?

In case he was knocked out cold.

How did the boxer describe her road to the title fight?

Rocky.

What did the boxers call their band?
The Ring Tones.

Where did boxers fight in the Wild West?
The K.O. Corral.

What does a chef bring to a boxing match?
Pound cake.

Why did the boxer want dessert?
His legs had turned to Jell-O®.

When does a boxer get food at the stadium?
On the weigh-in.

How did the boxer hurt his hand in the kitchen?
Counterpunch.

Why was the losing boxer nicknamed Milky Way?
She saw stars.

Why was the wrestler the only one who could start a campfire?
He won every match.

HA HA HA HA HA HA HA HA

How do wrestlers hold onto the ropes?

With their *ring* fingers.

Why does it take sumo wrestlers so long to see the doctor?

They have double the wait.

What do you call it when a wrestler gets thrown over the ropes?

Out-of-the-ring toss.

What's a lizard's favorite sport?

Gecko-Roman wrestling.

Why did the running back learn karate?

He wanted to break a tackle.

What sport lets you go in like a lion and out like a lamb?

The March-ial arts.

What do you call it when an athlete gains muscle but turns green?

Hulking up.

Why did the athlete go to the junkyard?

So she could trash talk.

They Coulda Been Contenders

When is a carpenter like an Olympic athlete?

When he throws his hammer.

When is a boxer like a farmer?

When he throws a haymaker.

When is an artist like a basketball player?

When she's in the paint.

When is a barber like a good athlete?

When he makes the cut.

When is a weaver like a shooting guard?

When she makes a basket.

When is a mail carrier like a wide receiver?

When he runs a post route.

When is a boxer like a carpenter?

When she's tough as nails.

When is a camper like a football recruiter?

When he's a Scout.

When is a race-car driver like a cat drinking milk?

When he's on the last lap.

WHAT'S THAT RACKET?

Where does a tennis player have a weak serve?

Wimp-ledon.

What do you call a female tennis player from Los Angeles?

A Volley Girl.

What's the best stroke in doubles tennis?

Forehand.

Why does tennis cost so much?

They even charge the net.

Why do waiters play tennis?

They like to serve.

HA HA HA HA HA HA HA

Why did the line judge tell the tennis players to settle down?

She wanted order on the court.

What does a tennis player call a sharp, burning pain?

Match point.

THE SPIRITS OF COMPETITION

Why did the college put ghosts on the cheerleading squad?

They had school spirit.

What do you get when you cross a ghost with an eagle?

A boo bird.

What do you call a ghost with her arms up in the air?

Ghoul posts.

Why was the ghost so good at basketball?

She had a great fade away.

How do spirits win every soccer game?

With ghost goals.

Why do ghosts make lousy sports fans?

They always boo.

What does a ghost say when his favorite team scores?

"Ghoooooooooooouuuuuuuulll!"

How did the ghost get on base?

With a boo-per.

Why can't ghosts play catch?

The ball goes right through them.

Why do mummies make great cheerleaders?

They can build pyramids.

What's a zombie's favorite soccer call?

Dead ball.

What's a zombie's best weightlifting event?

The dead lift.

What's a vampire's best weightlifting event?

The undead lift.

Did you hear about the boxer knocked out by Dracula?

He went down for the count.

What do you call it when Dracula eats too much at a baseball game?

A full count.

What kind of race scares a vampire?

Cross country.

Why was the vampire such a good punter?

His kicks had great fang time.

Why are vampires so competitive?

They play for blood.

Why was the Phantom of the Opera such a good football player?

He had his own face mask.

Why couldn't the Headless Horseman win a race?

He couldn't get ahead.

Where do you see ghosts fight?

Pay-per-boo.

HOLIDAY CHEERS

How does Santa kick a football?
With his mistletoe.

Why was Cupid so bad at tennis?
He lost every game 40-love.

Where's the best place to bowl
on Saint Patrick's Day?
Bowling Green.

How does Rudolph score 100 points in the
Reindeer Games?
He lights up the scoreboard.

How does a football team lose on Thanksgiving?
They get stuffed at the line of scrimmage.

Why did Santa cancel the game?
Rein-delay.

HA HA HA HA HA

What do you call it when Santa starts a race in first place?

The North Pole position.

How does a football coach sign Valentine's Day cards?

XOXOXO.

What does a racehorse celebrate every May?

Mudder's Day.

What does a racehorse celebrate every June?

Fodder's Day.

THE (NOT SO) BIG LEAGUES

Where do giants play?

The Big Leagues.

What's the worst name for a pee-wee football team?

The Giants.

Why don't elephants play football?

They don't make helmets that big.

Why do giants make such good wide receivers?

They can go long.

Why do whales make such good wide receivers?

They can go deep.

Why didn't the elf team win the big game?

They came up short.

Why don't elves hit home runs?

Because they play small ball.

Where do you find an elf in a basketball game?

The low post.

Why wouldn't the elf play college sports?

Because he knows he'll never be the big man on campus.

Why did the coach send an elf into the game?

He needed short yardage.

Where do elves first start playing football?

In Pee-Wee Leagues.

HA HA HA HA HA HA HA HA

THAT'S MY TEAM

Where do stadiums have the smallest drinks?

Minnesota.

Where do teams have the cleanest uniforms?

New Jersey.

What state can't hit a baseball?

Miss-again.

What do you call a baseball team that doesn't know anybody?

The Texas Strangers.

Which team always has a place to hang its uniforms?

The Cubbies.

What do you call a team of old ballplayers in Los Angeles?

The L.A. Codgers.

How would people feel if Houston won the World Series?

Astro-nomical.

Which team is black and white and rolls around the field?

The Baltimore Oreos.

Where do the Yankees keep their trophies?

On the Mickey Mantle.

Why were the Yankees so mean after Babe Ruth retired?

They were Ruth-less.

Why can't a Philadelphia football player get sick during a game?

That would be an ill-Eagle formation.

Which college team storms the field?

The Hurricanes.

Why don't the New Jersey Devils play baseball?

They'd never beat the Angels.

Which team is never chill?

The [Calgary] Flames.

What do you call a Houston basketball player with a sunburn?

Rockets' red glare.

Which team can't play night games?

The [Phoenix] Suns.

Why don't the [Sacramento] Kings ever win an afternoon game?

They prefer knight games.

Why don't basketball teams play in the kitchen?

They can't stand the [Miami] Heat.

Knock, knock!

Who's there?

Man U.

Man U. who?

Man U. should open this door!

KNOCK-KNOCK!

HA HA HA HA HA

How did the high-school quarterback hurt his math teacher?

He hit him in the numbers.

Where do chickens play college football?

Hen State.

What's the worst college bowl to play in?

The Toilet Bowl.

Why did the boxer play college football?

He wanted to play in the Punch Bowl.

Why do college teams sell so many jerseys in the spring?

It's Merch Madness!

Why did the college athlete have such good manners?

She had class.

HA HA HA HA HA

Why did the school kick the quarterback off the team?

He passed everything but his classes.

Knock, knock!

Who's there?

OU.

OU who?

OU, would you open the door already?!

KNOCK-KNOCK!

Knock, knock!

Who's there?

OSU.

OSU who?

OSU. I was expecting someone else.

BORN ATHLETES

What's a great name for a basketball player?

Duncan.

What's a great name for a baseball player?

Homer.

What's a great name for a bowler?

Lane.

What's a great name for a beach volleyball player?

Sandy.

What's a great name for a goalie?

Annette.

THE FARM LEAGUE

How do sheep win at sports?

They bleat the other team.

What's a sheep's favorite sport?

Baaaa-sketball.

Why aren't pigs good at team sports?

They're ball hogs.

Why does it cost so much to race pigs?

They're gas hogs.

HA HA HA HA HA HA HA HA

How do rabbits feel when they lose a game?

They don't carrot all.

Why are rabbits so good at basketball?

They have a great jump shot.

What's a rabbit's favorite position in baseball?

Shorthop.

Where do you keep a bull when you don't want him to charge?

A *stay-bull.*

What kind of bull scares a rodeo rider?

A bull elephant.

What do cowboys sing in the Land of Oz?

"Ro-de-o, yo ho."

HA HA HA HA HA HA HA HA

What do you call a farmer who picks up the most hay bales?

Most Valuable Hayer.

What did the farmer say to the cow when she got too old to play ball?

"You're *pasture* prime."

Why was the farmer such a lousy pitcher?

She threw bean balls.

What did the farmer say to his injured chicken?

"Balk it off."

Why are baby chicks such good athletes?

They're in peep condition.

How did the scarecrow end up in the Big Leagues?

He got called up from the farm team.

What do you call two mushrooms boxing?

Sporing partners.

What do you call a duck in the Arctic?

A fowl pole.

Why do chickens sit along the basepaths?

So they can catch fowl balls.

Why did the football player get rid of his pet chicken?

It was a personal *fowl*.

Why do chickens like basketball?

They always make the fowl shot.

Why was the flock of geese thrown out of the game?

Too many fowls.

What do you call a nice-smelling bird?

A fragrant fowl.

Why are chickens such bad umpires?

They call every pitch a "Balk!"

What kind of dog does a quarterback have?

A golden receiver.

Which dogs can't you wrestle with?

Boxers.

Why did the dogs link tails at the big game?

They wanted to tailgate.

Why are dogs so bad at sports?

They roll over.

What do you call a dog that's good at volleyball?

Spike.

How do cats play soccer?

With a fur ball.

Why can't cats be umpires?

They always say "Me-OWT!"

How did the cat win the race?

By a whisker.

WILD WORLD OF SPORTS

Why can't gorillas win at sports?

They only beat their chests.

What's an owl's favorite game?

Hoola-hoots.

What do cheerleading owls say?

"*Hoo*-ray!"

Why can't birds be heavyweights?

Because they're featherweights.

Why are red-breasted birds the best at baseball?
They're always *robin* you of a hit.

What do you call a race where you jump over tortoises?
The 100-meter turtle.

How does a skunk defend itself?
With kung-pew.

Which sea creature never scores in basketball?
A shrimp.

Which slimy creature is a great home-run hitter?
A *slug*-ger.

Why do octopuses make such good baseball players?
Because one player gives you a pitcher and seven relievers.

Why do rodents make risky football coaches?

They always want to *gopher* two.

What do you call a wild animal in the middle of a football field?

Fifty-yard lion.

Why don't dolphins make errors in baseball?

Because they do everything on porpoise.

How do you play a pick-up game with dolphins?

Shirts versus fins.

How did the kangaroo act when she got lost?

Hopping mad.

What do you call it when a kangaroo hops up and down in a basketball game?

Re-bounce.

Why don't kangaroos play the infield?

They're afraid of bad hops.

Why are blue jays so good at golf?

They always make a birdie.

Why did the fly race around the room?

He wanted to enter the Daytona Flyve Hundred.

When did the bumblebee win the basketball game?

At the buzzer.

HA HA HA

Why did the insects build their hive on the carpet?

So they could play rug-bee.

Why did the spider try out for the baseball team?

She wanted to catch flies.

Why are raccoons the last ones to enter the game?

They only play during garbage time.

How did the mouse win the big game?

In a squeaker.

What do monkeys sing when they win the big game?

"We Are the Chimp-ions."

What did the basketball player take fishing?

Nothing but net.

Which football player should you take fishing?

Tackle.

Why can't fishermen draw circles?

They're anglers.

When do hockey players go hunting?

Puck season.

Why did the running back learn to hunt?

So he could shoot the gap.

Why did the hunter sneak up on his dessert?

He was hunting mousse.

What sport is great on a hot day?

Iced-tee ball.

Why are mountain climbers in great shape?

They're at their physical peak.

Why do trees make such terrific baseball fans?

Because they root, root, root
for the home team!

Which season is never on the calendar?

Pre-season.

What kind of canoe does a baseball player
use to cross a lake?

Dugout.

What's the only season that sees flowers bloom
and leaves fall?

Baseball season.

Knock, knock!

Who's there?

Bass fish.

Bass fish who?

Bass fish I ever caught was with you.

Knock, knock!

Who's there?

Debate.

Debate who?

Debate is how we catch de fish.

THAT GUY'S A BEAST!

What does T. rex eat while camping?

Dino-s'mores.

Why did the dinosaur run downhill?

If you weighed 10,000 pounds,
would you run uphill?

What do you call a T. rex who gets hurt playing ball?

Dino-sore.

Which dinosaur swims, bikes, and runs in a race?

Tricerathon.

How does a stegosaurus steal second?

With his spikes up.

How does a stegosaurus hit a volleyball?

She spikes it.

What happened when Bigfoot tried to kick a football?

He mythed.

What do monsters call a pass behind the line of scrimmage?

A scream play.

Why didn't Cerberus play baseball?

There are no triple headers.

What position does Cyclops play in football?

I-back.

What position does a half-man, half-horse play?

Centaur-field.

What award do you give a knight that kills a dragon?

Most Valuable Slayer.

FAST TRACK FUNNIES

What makes left turns at 200 miles per hour and loves you very much?

A NasCare Bear.

Why are race-car drivers so good at football?

They put together a winning drive.

Why was the race-car driver so successful?

She was on the fast track.

Why did the race-car driver refuse to apologize for the accident?

His suit was blame-retardant.

How did the basketball player crash the race car?

She tried a no look pass.

Why are race-car drivers good at basketball?

They crash the boards.

Why did the old race-car driver make a pit stop?

He needed to re-tire.

What do you call it when a race-car driver tries on a new suit?

A fit stop.

Why does the Indy 500 make babies thirsty?

It's Formula One.

Why does hydrogen win every race?

No one wants to pass gas.

HA HA HA HA HA HA HA HA

What do you call the devil in a race car?

A speed demon.

Why did the fool bring his horse to church?

To win the steeplechase.

How do so many animals get hurt at the Kentucky Derby?

Horsin' around.

Where do racehorses get muddy?

The Kentucky Dirty.

Knock, knock!

Who's there?

Derby.

Derby who?

Derby comes before der C.

What's a racehorse's favorite gait?

The starting gate.

Which horse always comes up short in a race?

A pony.

Why don't horses race in the dark?

Because that would be a night mare.

How did the skater get cut?

With a roller*blade*.

Where does a rollerblader stand?

Inline.

Knock, knock!

Who's there?

Papa.

Papa who?

Papa wheelie on your bike.

HA

What did the young biker say when she played soccer?

"Look, Ma, no hands!"

How did the cyclist win the Tour de France?

On de bike.

What do you call a bike rider who gets burned at the Tour de France?

French toast.

What race gives the winner a pair of bicycle shorts?

The Tour de Pants.

Alley Oops

Why are bowlers such bad drivers?

They keep changing lanes.

Why are bowlers quiet?

They want to hear a pin drop.

What sport requires a debit card?

Bowling, because you need a PIN.

Why was the bowler in such good shape?

He had a six-pack.

Why was the bowling ball dirty?

It was in the gutter.

What did the bowler call her convenience store?

7–10.

Why didn't the bowler worry about a flat tire?

She picked up a spare.

FOOL-COURT PRESS

Why did the fool think he couldn't play quarterback?

Because he couldn't pass anything.

Why did the fool join the football team?

So he could be the tackling dummy.

Why did the fool bring her camera to the racetrack?

In case it was a photo finish.

Why did the fool dig a hole at the racetrack?

So cars could make a *pit* stop.

Why did the fool take a pig to the stock car race?

To hear the tires squeal.

Why did the fool wear tap shoes to go fishing?

For click bait.

Why did the fool think her horse had three heads?

She won the Triple Crown.

Why did the fool play golf in his kitchen?
    He wanted to sink the putt.

Why did the fool bring extra money to the ballpark?
    In case she had to tip her cap.

Why did the fool buy two theater tickets?
    He wanted to see a double play.

Why did the fool give the winners rotten fruit?
    To the victor go the spoils.

Why did the fool make her gym out of rocks?
    She wanted to train hard.

Why did the fool drink soda on his way to the trainer?
    He wanted to pass the fizz-ical.

Why did the fool think her friend was a game?
    She was a good sport.

Why did the clown join the basketball team?
    So he could be the court jester.

Why did the fool wear flip-flops to beach volleyball?

> He wanted a blowout.

Why did the fool remove the tongues from her shoes?

> So they wouldn't taste *de-feat*.

Why did the fool ride his bike twice a day?

> He wanted to re-cycle.

Why did the fool refuse to sit at the ballgame?

> Because she was in the stands.

Why did the fool sit in his room instead of going to the ballpark?

> It was a home game.

Why did the fool watch sports in the basement?

> His team was in the cellar.

HA HA HA HA HA HA HA HA HA HA

THOSE ARE SPORTS TERMS?

Bet you didn't know these words were sports terms, but we can prove it!

Lasso.
My team finished lasso they won't be in the playoffs.

Manatee.
Manatee-m that slow will never win.

Banter.
We need to banter-gether or we'll never win.

Eclipse.
Eclipse the receiver one more time, and he's outta the game!

Garden.
The garden tackle lead the way.

Goatee.

Goatee off at the golf course.

Europe.

Europe cattle in a rodeo.

Twilight.

If you can't play in the dark, twilight games.

Erased.

Erased around the track in a hurry.

Pastor.

Pastor at the finish line.

Esteem.

Esteem finished behind our team.

Waterway.

Waterway to win the game!

KEEPING SCORE

Knock, knock!
   Who's there?
Pennant.
   Pennant who?
I need pennant paper to keep score.

KNOCK-
KNOCK!

Who records injuries at a football game?
   The sorekeeper.

What's a mushroom's job at the ballpark?
   Sporekeeper.

Why did the golfer bury her scorecard?
   The lowest score wins.

What do you call numbers on a crate?
   A box score.

Why didn't the reporter like hockey players?
   She couldn't warm up to them.

Why was the reporter so good at covering jai alai?

He always got the scoop.

Why did the announcer hold the phone away from her ear after the race?

It was too close to call.

Why did the team's P.A. announcer get so many visitors?

He had a public address.

Why didn't the halfback stop for questions?

He was on the run.

What do you call a part-time sportscaster?

A day-by-day announcer.

HA HA HA
HA HA HA
HA HA
HA HA HA HA

Sports Headlines

Avalanche Win in Landslide

Twins Win Doubleheader

Kings Crowned Champions

Wizards Win on Trick Shot

Giants Land Big Trade

Blues Sad After Loss

Suns on Fire This Year

Pistons Pumped for Next Game

LOL-YMPICS

Why were the weightlifter's legs so weak?
He couldn't do squat.

What do you call a champion skeet shooter?
A shooting star.

What kind of gum does a javelin thrower like?
Spear-mint.

Why was Midas such a terrible Olympic judge?
Every medal turned to gold.

What do gymnasts wear when they get older?
Expand-ex.

Why did the gymnast use a racket?
Because tennis a great score in gymnastics.

Why did the gymnast do sit-ups on a carpet?
She was doing her floor exercise.

HA HA HA HA HA

What substance does a gymnast put on her food every June?

Summer salt.

Why was the Olympic athlete so good at running, jumping, and kicking?

He had athlete's feet.

What's an astronaut's favorite sport on the moon?

The high jump.

Why are astronauts so good at gymnastics?

They stick the landing.

Why is Pinocchio the fastest puppet?

He wins every race by a nose.

What's the only track you can't race on?

The warning track.

Why are waves so good at track and field?

They take lots of laps.

Why did the track star carry playing cards?

She wanted to run with the pack.

Why did the foolish crooks bring a track star with them?

In case the bank kept the money in a pole vault.

What do track stars do on the phone?

Discus.

What do you call a runner with ships on his feet?

Fleet-footed.

Why did the sprinter make herself invisible?

She wanted to run like the wind.

What did the fencer say when she lost?

"Curses! Foiled again."

When do fencers play with their food?

When it's swordfish.

Why did the fencer stand on top of the palace soldiers?

He was en garde.

Why was the fencer so funny?

She had a sharp wit.

What game makes you smaller?

Squash.

Why don't cricket players eat honey?

They don't want a sticky wicket.

Did you hear about the cricket team that lost big?

They got crushed like a bug.

Knock, knock!

Who's there?

Sinker.

Sinker who?

Sinker swim, it's up to you.

KNOCK-KNOCK!

Which sport doesn't need a water boy?

Swimming.

How was the high diver's Broadway debut?

She made a splash!

Why did the swimmer quit?

He was in too deep.

HA HA HA HA HA

Why can't swimmers box?

They take a dive.

How did the swimmer quit?

He threw in the towel.

TOUGH COMPETITION

What's the difference between an astronaut and a boxer?

One counts down and the other goes down for the count.

HA

What's the difference between a chicken and a pitcher?

One bawks and the other balks.

What's the difference between a pick-up game and a library book?

One has a do-over and the other is overdue.

HA HA HA HA HA

What's the difference between Thanksgiving and a bowling tournament?

One has a Butterball and the other has a gutterball.

What's the difference between a knight and a 10-inning baseball game?

One fights a dragon and the other drags on.

What's the difference between a dog and a home-run hitter?

One slobbers and the other clobbers.

What's the difference between a dog and a runner at third?

One catches fleas and the other flees catchers.

What's the difference between a theater agent and a quarterback?

One books plays and the other has a playbook.

What's the difference between a child playing in the snow and a softball team?

One wears mittens and the other wears ten mitts.

What's the difference between a boxer and a sad clown?

One fights a bout and the other fights a pout.

What's the difference between a brick layer and a baseball player?

One uses mortar and the other uses more tar.

What's the difference between a frontier woodsman and a wrestler?

One is a mountain man and the other is a mountain of a man.

What's the difference between an average athlete and a boxer?

One is O.K., and the other is K.O.'d.

CAUGHT STEALING

Why did the cops arrest the boxer?

He took a punch.

How did the cops record the track star?

100-meter-dash cam.

Why can't cops stop hockey players?

Because hockey players never "Freeze!"

Where do police officers stand at a hockey game?

On the thin blue line.

Why did the cops arrest the hockey team?

They were in a shootout.

How did the cop know the runner was going to steal a base?

She had a good lead.

Why did the baseball player stop stealing bases?

The cops gave him *arrest*.

Why was the baseball player kicked out of the music store?

He stole a bass.

What do pirates sing when they win the big game?

"We ARRRRRRGGH the Champions."

How does a pirate captain make a basket?

With a hook shot.

How did the pirate captain steal second?

Hook slide.

Why did the second team out of the tunnel go home?

The first team took the field.

What do rich baseball players wear during the game?

A salary cap.

Which player has his own boat?

The captain.

Where did the team trainer put her boat?

The sports doc.

Why don't basketball players carry money?

They like free throws.

Why did the basketball player give up her credit card?

So she wouldn't charge.

Why did the team owner pray for rain?

He didn't like fair weather fans.

Where does a football team owner pay his players?

The spend zone.

Why did the baker become a sports star?

For the dough!

KNOCK, KNOCK, KNOCK-OUTS

Knock, knock!
> Who's there?

Too windy.
> Too windy who?

Too windy game we need more points.

Knock, knock!
> Who's there?

Sailor.
> Sailor who?

Sail or motor, let's go boating!

Knock, knock!
> Who's there?

Orion.
> Orion who?

Keep Orion the ball.

HA HA HA HA HA

Knock, knock!

Who's there?

Shutout.

Shutout who?

Shutout of your house again.

Knock, knock!

Who's there?

Ice cream.

Ice cream who?

Ice cream for the home team.

Knock, knock!

Who's there?

Trainer.

Trainer who?

Trainer bus, how are we getting to the game?

Knock, knock!

Who's there?

Koala.

Koala who?

Koala your friends—it's game time!

KNOCK-KNOCK!

HA HA HA HA HA

Knock, knock!
> Who's there?

Hero.
> Hero who?

Hero'd the winning horse.

Knock, knock!
> Who's there?

Solo.
> Solo who?

Our score is solo, we'll never win.

Knock, knock!
> Who's there?

John Wooden.
> John Wooden who?

John Wooden open the door for me. Will you?

Knock, knock!
> Who's there?

Canoe.
> Canoe who?

Canoe come out and play now?

HA HA HA HA HA

Knock, knock!
> Who's there?

Iron.
> Iron who?

Iron in a marathon.

Knock, knock!
> Who's there?

Atrophy.
> Atrophy who?

Atrophy would be nice if we win.

Knock, knock!
> Who's there?

Defense.
> Defense who?

De*fense* stops de ball.

Knock, knock!
> Who's there?

Utah.
> Utah who?

Utah-k a good game.

HA HA HA HA HA

Knock, knock!

Who's there?

Honor roll.

Honor roll who?

The winning team is honor roll.

Knock, knock!

Who's there?

Homer.

Homer who?

Homer away, we'll play anywhere.

Knock, knock!

Who's there?

Picnic.

Picnic who?

Picnic for captain of the team.

Knock, knock!

Who's there?

Watson.

Watson who?

Watson second.

HA HA HA HA HA

Knock, knock!

Who's there?

Mountain.

Mountain who?

Mountain Arabian horse to win the race.

Knock, knock!

Who's there?

FIFA.

FIFA who?

Did you bring the FIFA the game?

Knock, knock!

Who's there?

Socket.

Socket who?

Socket to 'em!

HA HA HA HA HA HA HA HA HA HA HA HA HA

And the Winner Is . . .

Jets Fly by Falcons

Lions Roar Past Jaguars

Chargers Shock Steelers

Thunder Roll Over Opponents

Giants Leap Over Rockies

Mariners Catch Marlins

Cowboys Win in Shootout

Suns Scorch Heat

Wizards Can't Handle Magic

EXTRA INNINGS

If you thought that was a lot of jokes, this book is going into extra innings!

Knock, knock!
Who's there?
Overtime.
Overtime who?
Overtime, it gets cold out here.

KNOCK-KNOCK!

What was the electrical socket's best play?
The outlet pass.

What sport do chimney sweeps play?
Sootball.

What sport can you play under a table?
Footsyball.

How did the athlete feel after eating too many energy bars?

Fuelish.

Who took the cheerleader to the ball?

No one. Cheerleaders aren't allowed on the field.

Why don't losing teams visit the White House?

Because they're in the doghouse.

Why do they sell hotdogs at baseball games?

Because cold dogs are for hockey.

Why doesn't an artist win or lose?

She prefers to draw.

Why did the sports star smash all her albums?

Records are made to be broken.

Why was the angry athlete so hot?

He turned off the fans.

How do you get a tie in sports?

Go to the store like everyone else.

What medicine should an athlete never take if she wants to win?

Tie-lynol.

Why is the sun the best athlete in the solar system?

It's the only star.

Why was the Jack of Hearts crazy?

He was a wild card.

Why did the new player collapse after a bad game?

That's the way the rookie crumbles.

HA HA HA HA
HA HA HA
HA
HA HA HA
HA HA HA

ABOUT THE AUTHOR

John Briggs is a veteran comedy writer whose jokes have appeared on TV, radio, and in print. He's also a former sports reporter who has combined his dual careers in a one-of-a-kind sports joke book. In addition to thousands of stand-up shows across the country, he once served as the opening act for HBO's *Young Young Comedians* talent search. The author of the humorous picture book *Leaping Lemmings!*, he's been making kids and grown-ups laugh for decades. John lives in upstate New York. Find out more at johnbriggsbooks.net.